The Key Facts™ on China

Essential Information on China
By Patrick W. Nee
The Internationalist®
www.internationalist.com

The Internationalist®

International Business, Investment, and Travel

Published by:

The Internationalist Publishing Company

96 Walter Street/ Suite 200

Boston, MA 02131, USA

Tel: 617-354-7722

www.internationalist.com

PN@internationalist.com

Copyright © 2015 by PWN

09232015

The Internationalist is a Registered Trademark. "Key Facts" and "The Internationalist Business Guides" are Trademarks of The Internationalist Publishing Company.

All Rights are reserved under International, Pan-American, and Pan-Asian Conventions. No part of this book may be reproduced in any form without the written permission of the publisher. All rights vigorously enforced

Table Of Contents

Chapter 1: Background

Chapter 2: Geography

Chapter 3: People and Society

Chapter 4: Government

Chapter 5: Economy

Chapter 6: Energy

Chapter 7: Communications

Chapter 8: Transportation

Chapter 9: Military

Chapter 10: Transnational Issues

Chapter 1: Background

For centuries China stood as a leading civilization, outpacing the rest of the world in the arts and sciences, but in the 19th and early 20th centuries, the country was beset by civil unrest, major famines, military defeats, and foreign occupation. After World War II, the communists under MAO Zedong established an autocratic socialist system that, while ensuring China's sovereignty, imposed strict controls over everyday life and cost the lives of tens of millions of people. After 1978, MAO's successor DENG Xiaoping and other leaders focused on market-oriented economic development and by 2000 output had quadrupled. For much of the population, living standards have improved dramatically and the room for personal choice has expanded, yet political controls remain tight. Since the early 1990s, China has increased its global outreach and participation in international organizations.

Chapter 2: Geography

Location:
> Eastern Asia, bordering the East China Sea, Korea Bay, Yellow Sea, and South China Sea, between North Korea and Vietnam

Geographic coordinates:
> 35 00 N, 105 00 E

Map references:
> Asia

Area:
> total: 9,596,960 sq km
> country comparison to the world: 4
> land: 9,326,410 sq km
> water: 270,550 sq km

Area - comparative:
> slightly smaller than the US

Land boundaries:
> total: 22,457 km
> border countries: Afghanistan 91 km, Bhutan 477 km, Burma 2,129 km, India 2,659 km, Kazakhstan 1,765 km, North Korea 1,352 km, Kyrgyzstan 1,063 km, Laos 475 km, Mongolia 4,630 km, Nepal 1,389 km, Pakistan 438 km, Russia (northeast) 4,133 km, Russia (northwest) 46 km, Tajikistan 477 km, Vietnam 1,297 km
> regional borders: Hong Kong 33 km, Macau 3 km

Coastline:
> 14,500 km

Maritime claims:
    territorial sea: 12 nm
    contiguous zone: 24 nm
    exclusive economic zone: 200 nm
    continental shelf: 200 nm or to the edge of the continental margin

Climate:
    extremely diverse; tropical in south to subarctic in north

Terrain:
    mostly mountains, high plateaus, deserts in west; plains, deltas, and hills in east

Elevation extremes:
    lowest point: Turpan Pendi -154 m
    highest point: Mount Everest 8,850 m

Natural resources:
    coal, iron ore, petroleum, natural gas, mercury, tin, tungsten, antimony, manganese, molybdenum, vanadium, magnetite, aluminum, lead, zinc, rare earth elements, uranium, hydropower potential (world's largest), arable land

Land use:
    agricultural land: 54.7%
    other: 23% (2011 est.)

Irrigated land:
    629,380 sq km (2006)

Total renewable water resources:
    2,840 cu km (2011)

Freshwater withdrawal (domestic/industrial/agricultural):
>total: 554.1 cu km/yr (12%/23%/65%)
>per capita: 409.9 cu m/yr (2005)

Natural hazards:
>frequent typhoons (about five per year along southern and eastern coasts); damaging floods; tsunamis; earthquakes; droughts; land subsidence
>>volcanism: China contains some historically active volcanoes including Changbaishan (also known as Baitoushan, Baegdu, or P'aektu-san), Hainan Dao, and Kunlun although most have been relatively inactive in recent centuries

Environment - current issues:
>air pollution (greenhouse gases, sulfur dioxide particulates) from reliance on coal produces acid rain; water shortages, particularly in the north; water pollution from untreated wastes; deforestation; estimated loss of one-fifth of agricultural land since 1949 to soil erosion and economic development; desertification; trade in endangered species

Environment - international agreements:
>party to: Antarctic-Environmental Protocol, Antarctic Treaty, Biodiversity, Climate Change, Climate Change-Kyoto Protocol, Desertification, Endangered Species, Environmental Modification, Hazardous Wastes, Law of the

Sea, Marine Dumping, Ozone Layer Protection, Ship Pollution, Tropical Timber 83, Tropical Timber 94, Wetlands, Whaling
<u>signed, but not ratified</u>: none of the selected agreements

Geography - note:
world's fourth largest country (after Russia, Canada, and US); Mount Everest on the border with Nepal is the world's tallest peak

Chapter 3: People and Society

Nationality:
    noun: Chinese (singular and plural)
    adjective: Chinese

Ethnic groups:
    Han Chinese 91.6%, Zhuang 1.3%, Manchu, Hui, Miao, Uighur, Tujia, Yi, Mongol, Tibetan, Buyi, Dong, Yao, Korean, and other nationalities 7.1% (2010census)

Languages:
    Standard Chinese or Mandarin (official; Putonghua, based on the Beijing dialect), Yue (Cantonese), Wu (Shanghainese), Minbei (Fuzhou), Minnan (Hokkien-Taiwanese), Xiang, Gan, Hakka dialects, minority languages (see Ethnic groups entry)
    note: Zhuang is official in Guangxi Zhuang, Yue is official in Guangdong, Mongolian is official in Nei Mongol, Uighur is official in Xinjiang Uygur, Kyrgyz is official in Xinjiang Uygur, and Tibetan is official in Xizang (Tibet)

Religions:
    Buddhist 18.2%, Christian 5.1%, Muslim 1.8%, folk religion 21.9%, Hindu < .1%, other 0.7% (includes Daoist (Taoist)), unaffiliated 52.2%
    note: officially atheist (2010 est.)

Population:
    1,367,485,388 (July 2015 est.)
    country comparison to the world: 1

Age structure:
    0-14 years: 17.08% (male 126,146,137/female 107,410,265)
    15-24 years: 13.82% (male 100,380,703/female 88,615,299)
    25-54 years: 47.95% (male 334,240,795/female 321,417,301)
    55-64 years: 11.4% (male 77,098,602/female 75,286,553)
    65 years and over: 10.01% (male 65,573,256/female 71,316,477) (2015 est.)

Median age:
    total: 36.7 years
    male: 35.8 years
    female: 37.5 years (2014 est.)

Population growth rate:
    0.45% (2015 est.)
    country comparison to the world: 159

Birth rate:
    12.49 births/1,000 population (2015 est.)
    country comparison to the world: 115

Death rate:
    7.53 deaths/1,000 population (2015 est.)
    country comparison to the world: 127

Net migration rate:
    -0.44 migrant(s)/1,000 population (2015 est.)
    country comparison to the world: 127

Urbanization:
    urban population: 55.6% of total population (2015)
    rate of urbanization: 3.05% annual rate of change (2010-15 est.)

Major cities - population:
Shanghai 23.741 million; BEIJING (capital) 20.384 million; Chongqing 13.332 million; Guangdong 12.548 million; Tianjin 11.21 million; Shenzhen 10.749 million (2015)

Sex ratio:
at birth: 1.15 male(s)/female
0-14 years: 1.17 male(s)/female
15-24 years: 1.13 male(s)/female
25-54 years: 1.04 male(s)/female
55-64 years: 1.02 male(s)/female
65 years and over: 0.92 male(s)/female
total population: 1.06 male(s)/female (2015 est.)

Infant mortality rate:
total: 12.44 deaths/1,000 live births
country comparison to the world: 121
male: 12.58 deaths/1,000 live births
female: 12.27 deaths/1,000 live births (2015 est.)

Life expectancy at birth:
total population: 75.41 years
country comparison to the world: 96
male: 73.38 years
female: 77.73 years (2015 est.)

Total fertility rate:
1.6 children born/woman (2015 est.)
country comparison to the world: 181

Health expenditures:
5.6% of GDP (2013)
country comparison to the world: 126

Physicians density:
1.49 physicians/1,000 population (2011)

Hospital bed density:
  3.8 beds/1,000 population (2011)
Sanitation facility access:
  improved:
    urban: 86.6% of population
    rural: 63.7% of population
    total: 76.5% of population
  unimproved:
    urban: 13.4% of population
    rural: 36.3% of population
    total: 23.5% of population

HIV/AIDS - adult prevalence rate:
  0.1% (2012 est.)
  country comparison to the world: 112
HIV/AIDS - people living with HIV/AIDS:
  780,000 (2012 est.)
  country comparison to the world: 11
HIV/AIDS - deaths:
  NA
Major infectious diseases:
  degree of risk: intermediate
  food or waterborne diseases: bacterial diarrhea, hepatitis A, and typhoid fever
  vectorborne diseases: Japanese encephalitis
  soil contact disease: hantaviral hemorrhagic fever with renal syndrome (HFRS)
  note: highly pathogenic H5N1 avian influenza has been identified in this country; it poses a negligible risk with extremely rare cases possible among US citizens who have close contact with birds (2013)

Obesity - adult prevalence rate:
    7.3% (2014)
    country comparison to the world: 152

Children under the age of 5 years underweight:
    3.4% (2010)
    country comparison to the world: 109

Literacy:
    definition: age 15 and over can read and write
    total population: 96.4%
    male: 98.2%
    female: 94.5% (2015)

School life expectancy (primary to tertiary education):
    total: 13 years
    male: 13 years
    female: 13 years (2009)

Chapter 4: Government

Country name:
  conventional long form: People's Republic of China
  conventional short form: China
  local long form: Zhonghua Renmin Gongheguo
  local short form: Zhongguo
  abbreviation: PRC
Government type:
  Communist state
Capital:
  name: Beijing
  geographic coordinates: 39 55 N, 116 23 E
  time difference: UTC+8 (13 hours ahead of Washington, DC during Standard Time)
  note: despite its size, all of China falls within one time zone; many people in Xinjiang Province observe an unofficial "Xinjiang time zone" of UTC+6, two hours behind Beijing
Administrative divisions:
  23 provinces (sheng, singular and plural), 5 autonomous regions (zizhiqu, singular and plural), and 4 municipalities (shi, singular and plural)
  provinces: Anhui, Fujian, Gansu, Guangdong, Guizhou, Hainan, Hebei, Heilongjiang, Henan, Hubei, Hunan, Jiangsu, Jiangxi, Jilin, Liaoning, Qinghai, Shaanxi, Shandong, Shanxi, Sichuan, Yunnan, Zhejiang; (see note on Taiwan)

autonomous regions: Guangxi, Nei Mongol (Inner Mongolia), Ningxia, Xinjiang Uygur, Xizang (Tibet)

municipalities: Beijing, Chongqing, Shanghai, Tianjin

note: China considers Taiwan its 23rd province; see separate entries for the special administrative regions of Hong Kong and Macau

Independence:
1 October 1949 (People's Republic of China established); notable earlier dates: 221 BC (unification under the Qin Dynasty); 1 January 1912 (Qing Dynasty replaced by the Republic of China)

National holiday:
Anniversary of the founding of the People's Republic of China, 1 October (1949)

Constitution:
most recent promulgation 4 December 1982; amended several times, last in 2004

Legal system:
civil law influenced by Soviet and continental European civil law systems; legislature retains power to interpret statutes; note - criminal procedure law revised in early 2012

International law organization participation:
has not submitted an ICJ jurisdiction declaration; non-party state to the ICCt

Suffrage:
18 years of age; universal

Executive branch:
chief of state: President XI Jinping (since 14 March 2013); Vice President Li Yuanchao (since 14 March 2013)
head of government: Premier LI Keqiang (since 16 March 2013); Executive Vice Premiers ZHANG Gaoli (since 16 March 2013), LIU Yandong (since 16 March 2013), MA Kai (since 16 March 2013), WANG Yang (since 16 March 2013)
cabinet: State Council appointed by National People's Congress
elections: president and vice president elected by National People's Congress for a five-year term (eligible for a second term); elections last held on 5-17 March 2013 (next to be held in March 2018); premier nominated by president, confirmed by National People's Congress
election results: XI Jinping elected president; National People's Congress vote – 2,952; LI Yuanchao elected vice president with 2,940 votes

Legislative branch:
unicameral National People's Congress or Quanguo Renmin Daibiao Dahui (2,987 seats; members elected by municipal, regional, and provincial people's congresses, and People's Liberation Army; members serve 5-year terms); note – in practice, only members of the Chinese Communist Party (CCP), its 8 allied parties, and CCP-approved independent candidaets are elected

elections: last held in December 2012-February 2013 (next to be held in late 2017 to early 2018) election results: percent of vote - NA; seats - 2,987

Judicial branch:
Supreme People's Court (judges appointed by the National People's Congress); Local People's Courts (comprise higher, intermediate, and basic courts); Special People's Courts (primarily military, maritime, railway transportation, and forestry courts)

Political parties and leaders:
Chinese Communist Party or CCP [XI Jinping]; eight nominally independent small parties ultimately controlled by the CCP

Political pressure groups and leaders:
no substantial political opposition groups exist

International organization participation:
ADB, AfDB (nonregional member), APEC, ARF, ASEAN (dialogue partner), BIS, CDB, CICA, EAS, FAO, FATF, G-20, G-24 (observer), G-77, IADB, IAEA, IBRD, ICAO, ICC (national committees), ICRM, IDA, IFAD, IFC, IFRCS, IHO, ILO, IMF, IMO, IMSO, Interpol, IOC, IOM (observer), IPU, ISO, ITSO, ITU, LAIA (observer), MIGA, MINURSO, MONUSCO, NAM (observer), NSG, OAS (observer), OPCW, PCA, PIF (partner), SAARC (observer), SCO, SICA (observer), UN, UNAMID, UNCTAD, UNESCO, UNFICYP, UNHCR, UNIDO, UNIFIL, UNISFA, UNMIL, UNMISS, UNMIT, UNOCI, UNSC (permanent),

UNTSO, UNWTO, UPU, WCO, WHO, WIPO, WMO, WTO, ZC

Diplomatic representation in the US:
chief of mission: Ambassador CUI Tiankai (since 3 April 2013)
chancery: 3505 International Place NW, Washington, DC 20008
telephone: [1] (202) 495-2266
FAX: [1] (202) 495-2190
consulate(s) general: Chicago, Houston, Los Angeles, New York, San Francisco

Diplomatic representation from the US:
chief of mission: Ambassador Max Sieben BAUCUS (since 18 March 2014)
embassy: 55 An Jia Lou Lu, 100600 Beijing
mailing address: PSC 461, Box 50, FPO AP 96521-0002
telephone: [86] (10) 8531-3000
FAX: [86] (10) 8531-3300
consulate(s) general: Chengdu, Guangzhou, Shanghai, Shenyang, Wuhan

Flag description:
red with a large yellow five-pointed star and four smaller yellow five-pointed stars (arranged in a vertical arc toward the middle of the flag) in the upper hoist-side corner; the color red represents revolution, while the stars symbolize the four social classes - the working class, the peasantry, the urban petty bourgeoisie, and the national bourgeoisie (capitalists) - united under the Communist Party of China

National symbol(s):
dragon; national colors: red, yellow
National anthem:
name: "Yiyongjun Jinxingqu" (The March of the Volunteers)
lyrics/music: TIAN Han/NIE Er
note: adopted 1949; the anthem, though banned during the Cultural Revolution, is more commonly known as "Zhongguo Guoge" (Chinese National Song); it was originally the theme song to the 1935 Chinese movie, "Sons and Daughters in a Time of Storm"

Chapter 5: Economy

Economy - overview:
Since the late 1970s China has moved from a closed, centrally planned system to a more market-oriented one that plays a major global role – in 2010 China became the world's largest exporter. Reforms began with the phasing out of collectivized agriculture, and expanded to include the gradual liberalization of prices, fiscal decentralization, inc reased autonomy for state enterprises, growth of the private sector, development of stock markets and a mdoern banking system, and opening to foreign trade and investment. China has implemented reforms in a gradualist fashion. In recent years, China has renewed its support for state-owned enterprises in sectors considered important to "economic security," explicitly looking to foster globally competitive industries. The restructuring of the economy and resulting efficiency gains have contributed to a more than tenfold increase in GDP since 1978. Measured on a purchasing power parity (PPP) basis that adjusts for price differences, China in 2014 stood as the largest economy in the world, surpassing the US for the first time in modern history. Still, China's per capita income is below the world average.

After keeping its currency tightly linked to the US dollar for years, in July 2005 China moved to an exchange rate system that references a basket of curencies. From mid 2005 to late 2008 cumulative appreciation of the renminbi against the US dollar was more than 20%, but the exchange rate remained virtually pegged to the dollar from the onset of the global financial crisis until June 2010, when Beijing allowed resumption of a gradual appreciation. In 2014 the People's Bank of China (PBOC) doubled the daily trading band within the RMB is permitted to fluctuate.

The Chinese government faces numerous economic challenges, including: (a) reducing its high domestic savings rate and correspondingly low domestic consumption; (b) facilitating higher-wage job opportunities for the aspiring middle class, including rural migrants and increasing numbers of college graduates; (c) reducing corruption and other economic crimes; and (d0 containing environmental damage and social strife related to the economy's rapid transformation. Economic development has progressed further in coastal provinces than in the interior, and by 2014 more than 274 millino migrant workers and their dependents ahd relocated to urban areas to find work. One consequence of population control policy is that china is now one of the most rapidly aging countries int eh world. Deterioration in the government – notably air pollution, soil erosion, and the steady fall fo the water table, especially in the North – is another long-term problem. China continues to lose arable land because fo erosion and economic development. The chinese government is seeking to add energy production capacity from sources other than coal and oil, focusing on nuclear and alternative energy development.

Several factors are converging to slow China's growth, including debt overhang from its credit-fueled stimulus program, industrial overcapcity, inefficient allocation of capital by state-owned banks, and the slow recovery of China's trading partners. The government's 12th Five-Year Plan, adopted in March 201 and reiterated at the Communist Party's "Third Plenum" meeting in November 20213, emphasizes continued economic reforms and the need to increase domestic consumption in order to make the economy less dependent in the future on fixed investments, exports, and heavy industry. However, China has made only marginal progress toward these rebalancing goals. The new government of President XI Jinping has signaled a greater willingness to udnertake reforms that focus on China's long-term economic health, including giving the market a more decisive role in allocating resources. In 2014 China agreed to begin limiting carbon dioxide emissions by 2030. China also implemented several economic reforms in 2014, including passing legislation to allow local governments to issue bonds, opening several state-owned enterprises to further prviate investment, loosening the one-child policy, passing harsher pollution fines, and cutting administrative red tape.

GDP (purchasing power parity):
$17.62 trillion (2014 est.)
country comparison to the world: 1
$16.41 trillion (2013 est.)
$15.23 trillion (2012 est.)
note: data are in 2012 US dollars

GDP (official exchange rate):
$10.38 trillion
note: because China's exchange rate is determine by fiat, rather than by market forces, the official exchange rate measure of GDP is not an accurate measure of China's output; GDP at the official exchange rate substantially understates the actual level of China's output vis-a-vis the rest of the world; in China's situation, GDP at purchasing power parity provides the best measure for comparing output across countries (2014 est.)

GDP - real growth rate:
7.4% (2014 est.)
country comparison to the world: 14
7.8% (2013 est.)
7.8% (2012 est.)

GDP - per capita (PPP):
$12,900 (2014 est.)
country comparison to the world: 113
$12,000 (2013 est.)
$11,100 (2012 est.)
note: data are in 2014 US dollars

GDP - composition by sector:
    agriculture: 9.2%
    industry: 42.6%
    services: 48.2% (2014 est.)

Labor force:
    801.6 million
    country comparison to the world: 1
    note: by the end of 2012, population at working age (15-64 years) was 1.004 billion (2014 est.)

Labor force - by occupation:
    agriculture: 33.6%
    industry: 30.3%
    services: 36.1% (2012 est.)

Unemployment rate:
    4.1% (2014 est.)
    country comparison to the world: 36
    4.1% (2013 est.)
    note: data are for registered urban unemployment, which excludes private enterprises and migrants

Population below poverty line:
    6.1%
    note: in 2011, China set a new poverty line at RMB 2300 (approximately US $400)
    (2013 est.)

Household income or consumption by percentage share:
    lowest 10%: 1.7%
    highest 10%: 30%
    note: data are for urban households only (2009)

Distribution of family income - Gini index:
>46.9 (2014 est.)
>country comparison to the world: 26
>47.3 (2013 est.)

Budget:
>revenues: $2.285 trillion
>expenditures: $2.469 trillion (2014 est.)

Taxes and other revenues:
>22.1% of GDP (2014 est.)
>country comparison to the world: 145

Budget surplus (+) or deficit (-):
>-1.8% of GDP (2014 est.)
>country comparison to the world: 112

Public debt:
>15.1% of GDP (2014 est.)
>country comparison to the world: 137
>15.3% of GDP (2013 est.)
>note: official data; data cover both central government debt and local government debt, which China's National Audit Office estimated at RMB 10.72 trillion (approximately US$1.66 trillion) in 2011; data exclude policy bank bonds, Ministry of Railway debt, China Asset Management Company debt, and non-performing loans

Inflation rate (consumer prices):
>2% (2014 est.)
>country comparison to the world: 100
>2.6% (2013 est.)

Central bank discount rate:
    2.25% (31 December 2014 est.)
    country comparison to the world: 115
    2.25% (31 December 2013 est.)

Commercial bank prime lending rate:
    5.6% (31 December 2014 est.)
    country comparison to the world: 132
    6. % (31 December 2013 est.)

Stock of narrow money:
    $5.667 trillion (31 December 2014 est.)
    country comparison to the world: 2
    $5.528 trillion (31 December 2013 est.)

Stock of broad money:
    $20 trillion (31 December 2014 est.)
    country comparison to the world: 1
    $18.13 trillion (31 December 2013 est.)

Stock of domestic credit:
    $13.3 trillion (31 December 2014 est.)
    country comparison to the world: 3
    $15.19 trillion (31 December 2013 est.)

Market value of publicly traded shares:
    $6.065trillion (31 December 2014 est.)
    country comparison to the world: 3
    $6.499 trillion (31 December 2013)
    $5.753 trillion (31 December 2012 est.)

Agriculture - products:
    world leader in gross value of agricultural output; rice, wheat, potatoes, corn, peanuts, tea, millet, barley, apples, cotton, oilseed; pork; fish

Industrial production growth rate:
    7% (2014 est.)
    country comparison to the world: 27

Current account balance:
    $219.7 billion (2014 est.)
    country comparison to the world: 2
    $182.8 billion (2013 est.)

Exports:
    $2.343 trillion (2014 est.)
    country comparison to the world: 1
    $2.209 trillion (2013 est.)

Exports - commodities:
    electrical and other machinery, including data processing equipment, apparel, furniture, textiles, integrated circuits

Exports - partners:
    US 16.9%, Hong Kong 15.5%, Japan 6.4%, South Korea 4.3% (2014 est.)

Imports:
    $1.96 trillion (2014 est.)
    country comparison to the world: 3
    $1.95 trillion (2013 est.)

Imports - commodities:
    electrical and other machinery, oil and mineral fuels; nuclear reactor, boiler, and machinery components; optical and medical equipment, metal ores, motor vehicles; soybeans

Imports - partners:
    South Korea 9.7%, Japan 8.3%, US 8.1%, Taiwan 7.8%, Germany 5.4%, Australia 5% (2014 est.)

Reserves of foreign exchange and gold:
    $3.899 trillion (31 December 2014 est.)
    country comparison to the world: 1
    $3.88 trillion (31 December 2013 est.)

Debt - external:
$894.9 billion (31 December 2014 est.)
country comparison to the world: 17
$863.2 billion (31 December 2013 est.)
Stock of direct foreign investment - at home:
$1.287 trillion (31 December 2014 est.)
country comparison to the world: 5
$956.8 billion (31 December 2013 est.)
Stock of direct foreign investment - abroad:
$646.3 billion (31 December 2014 est.)
country comparison to the world: 12
$613.6 billion (31 December 2013 est.)
Exchange rates:
Renminbi yuan (RMB) per US dollar –
6.1428 (2014 est.)
6.1958 (2013 est.)
6.311 (2012 est.)
6.4615 (2011 est.)
6.7703 (2010 est.)
Fiscal year:
calendar year

Chapter 6: Energy

Electricity - production:
    5.65 trillion kWh (2014)
    country comparison to the world: 1

Electricity - consumption:
    5.523 trillion kWh (2014)
    country comparison to the world: 1

Electricity - exports:
    18.16 billion kWh (2014)
    country comparison to the world: 9

Electricity - imports:
    6.75 billion kWh (2014)
    country comparison to the world: 33

Electricity - installed generating capacity:
    1.505 billion kW (2014 est.)
    country comparison to the world: 1

Electricity - from fossil fuels:
    67.3% of total installed capacity (2014 est.)
    country comparison to the world: 111

Electricity - from nuclear fuels:
    1.5% of total installed capacity (2014 est.)
    country comparison to the world: 31

Electricity - from hydroelectric plants:
    22.2% of total installed capacity (2014 est.)
    country comparison to the world: 88

Electricity - from other renewable sources:
    9% of total installed capacity (2014 est.)
    country comparison to the world: 45

Crude oil - production:
    4.202 million bbl/day (2014 est.)
    country comparison to the world: 4

Crude oil - exports:
>12,000 bbl/day (2014 est.)
>country comparison to the world: 55

Crude oil - imports:
>6.167 million bbl/day (2014 est.)
>country comparison to the world: 2

Crude oil - proved reserves:
>18.1 billion bbl (1 January 2014 est.)
>country comparison to the world: 14

Refined petroleum products - production:
>9.648 million bbl/day (2013 est.)
>country comparison to the world: 3

Refined petroleum products - consumption:
>10.76 million bbl/day (2013 est.)
>country comparison to the world: 3

Refined petroleum products - exports:
>593,400 bbl/day (2014 est.)
>country comparison to the world: 12

Refined petroleum products - imports:
>600,000 bbl/day (2014 est.)
>country comparison to the world: 5

Natural gas - production:
>130.2 billion cu m (2014 est.)
>country comparison to the world: 7

Natural gas - consumption:
>181.8 billion cu m (2014 est.)
>country comparison to the world: 5

Natural gas - exports:
>2.647 billion cu m (2014 est.)
>country comparison to the world: 36

Natural gas - imports:
    58 billion cu m (2014 est.)
    country comparison to the world: 6
Natural gas - proved reserves:
    3.3 trillion cu m (1 January 2014 est.)
    country comparison to the world: 11
Carbon dioxide emissions from consumption of energy:
    10 billion Mt (2013 est.)
    country comparison to the world: 1

Chapter 7: Communications

Telephones – fixed lines:
  249.4 million (2014 est.)
  country comparison to the world: 1
Telephones - mobile cellular:
  1.3 billion (2011)
  country comparison to the world: 1
Telephone system:
  general assessment: domestic and international services are increasingly available for private use; unevenly distributed domestic system serves principal cities, industrial centers, and many towns; China continues to develop its telecommunications infrastructure, and is partnering with foreign providers to expand its global reach; China in the summer of 2008 began a major restructuring of its telecommunications industry, resulting in the consolidation of its six telecom service operators to three, China Telecom, China Mobile and China Unicom, each providing both fixed-line and mobile services
  domestic: interprovincial fiber-optic trunk lines and cellular telephone systems have been installed; mobile-cellular subscribership is increasing rapidly; the number of Internet users exceeded 564 million by the end of 2012; a domestic satellite system with several earth stations is in place
  international: country code - 86; a number of submarine cables provide connectivity to Asia,

the Middle East, Europe, and the US; satellite earth stations - 7 (5 Intelsat - 4 Pacific Ocean and 1 Indian Ocean; 1 Intersputnik - Indian Ocean region; and 1 Inmarsat - Pacific and Indian Ocean regions) (2012)

Broadcast media:
all broadcast media are owned by, or affiliated with, the Communist Party of China or a government agency; no privately-owned TV or radio stations; state-run Chinese Central TV, provincial, and municipal stations offer more than 2,000 channels; the Central Propaganda Department lists subjects that are off limits to domestic broadcast media with the government maintaining authority to approve all programming; foreign-made TV programs must be approved prior to broadcast

Internet country code:
.cn

Internet users:
626.6 million (2014 est.)
country comparison to the world: 1

Chapter 8:Transportation

Airports:
>507 (2013)
>country comparison to the world: 14

Airports - with paved runways:
>total: 463
>over 3,047 m: 71
>2,438 to 3,047 m: 158
>1,524 to 2,437 m: 123
>914 to 1,523 m: 25
>under 914 m: 86 (2013)

Airports - with unpaved runways:
>total: 44
>over 3,047 m: 4
>2,438 to 3,047 m: 7
>1,524 to 2,437 m: 6
>914 to 1,523 m: 9
>under 914 m: 18 (2013)

Heliports:
>47 (2013)

Pipelines:
>condensate 9 km; gas 48,502 km; oil 23,072 km; refined products 15,298 km; water 9 km (2013)

Railways:
>total: 191,270 km
>country comparison to the world: 3
>standard gauge: 190,000 km 1.435-m gauge (92,000 km electrified) (2014)

Roadways:
>total: 4,106,387 km
>country comparison to the world: 2

paved: 3,453,890 km (includes 84,946 km of expressways)
unpaved: 652,497 km (2011)

Waterways:
110,000 km (navigable waterways) (2011)
country comparison to the world: 1

Merchant marine:
total: 2,030
country comparison to the world: 3
by type: barge carrier 7, bulk carrier 621, cargo 566, carrier 10, chemical tanker 140, container 206, liquefied gas 60, passenger 9, passenger/cargo 81, petroleum tanker 264, refrigerated cargo 33, roll on/roll off 8, specialized tanker 2, vehicle carrier 23
foreign-owned: 22 (Hong Kong 18, Indonesia 2, Japan 2)
registered in other countries: 1,559 (Bangladesh 1, Belize 61, Cambodia 177, Comoros 1, Cyprus 6, Georgia 10, Honduras 2, Hong Kong 500, India 1, Indonesia 1, Kiribati 26, Liberia 4, Malta 6, Marshall Islands 14, North Korea 3, Panama 534, Philippines 4, Saint Kitts and Nevis 1, Saint Vincent and the Grenadines 65, Sao Tome and Principe 1, Sierra Leone 19, Singapore 29, South Korea 6, Thailand 1, Togo 1, Tuvalu 4, UK 7, Vanuatu 1, unknown 73) (2010)

Ports and terminals:
Dalian, Guangzhou, Ningbo, Qingdao, Qinhuangdao, Shanghai, Shenzhen, Tianjin

Chapter 9: Military

Military branches:
People's Liberation Army (PLA): Ground Forces, Navy (includes marines and naval aviation), Air Force (Zhongguo Renmin Jiefangjun Kongjun, PLAAF; includes Airborne Forces), and Second Artillery Corps (strategic missile force); People's Armed Police (PAP); PLA Reserve Force (2012)

Military service age and obligation:
18-24 years of age for selective compulsory military service, with a 2 year service obligation; no minimum age for voluntary service (all officers are volunteers); 18-19 years of age for women high school graduates who meet requirements for specific military jobs; a recent military decision allows women in combat roles; the first class of women warship commanders was in training in 2011 (2012)

Manpower available for military service:
males age 16-49: 385,821,101
females age 16-49: 363,789,674 (2010 est.)

Manpower fit for military service:
males age 16-49: 318,265,016
females age 16-49: 300,323,611 (2010 est.)

Manpower reaching militarily significant age annually:
male: 10,406,544
female: 9,131,990 (2010 est.)

Military expenditures:
1.99% of GDP (2012)
country comparison to the world: 40

Chapter 10: Transnational Issues

Disputes - international:
continuing talks and confidence-building measures work toward reducing tensions over Kashmir that nonetheless remains militarized with portions under the de facto administration of China (Aksai Chin), India (Jammu and Kashmir), and Pakistan (Azad Kashmir and Northern Areas); India does not recognize Pakistan's ceding historic Kashmir lands to China in 1964; China and India continue their security and foreign policy dialogue started in 2005 related to the dispute over most of their rugged, militarized boundary, regional nuclear proliferation, and other matters; China claims most of India's Arunachal Pradesh to the base of the Himalayas; lacking any treaty describing the boundary, Bhutan and China continue negotiations to establish a common boundary alignment to resolve territorial disputes arising from substantial cartographic discrepancies, the largest of which lie in Bhutan's northwest and along the Chumbi salient; Burmese forces attempting to dig in to the largely autonomous Shan State to rout local militias tied to the drug trade, prompts local residents to periodically flee into neighboring Yunnan Province in China; Chinese maps show an international boundary symbol off the coasts of the littoral states of the South China Seas,

where China has interrupted Vietnamese hydrocarbon exploration; China asserts sovereignty over Scarborough Reef along with the Philippines and Taiwan, and over the Spratly Islands together with Malaysia, the Philippines, Taiwan, Vietnam, and Brunei; the 2002 Declaration on the Conduct of Parties in the South China Sea eased tensions in the Spratlys but is not the legally binding code of conduct sought by some parties; Vietnam and China continue to expand construction of facilities in the Spratlys and in March 2005, the national oil companies of China, the Philippines, and Vietnam signed a joint accord on marine seismic activities in the Spratly Islands; China occupies some of the Paracel Islands also claimed by Vietnam and Taiwan; the Japanese-administered Senkaku Islands are also claimed by China and Taiwan; certain islands in the Yalu and Tumen rivers are in dispute with North Korea; North Korea and China seek to stem illegal migration to China by North Koreans, fleeing privations and oppression, by building a fence along portions of the border and imprisoning North Koreans deported by China; China and Russia have demarcated the once disputed islands at the Amur and Ussuri confluence and in the Argun River in accordance with their 2004 Agreement; China and Tajikistan have begun demarcating the revised boundary agreed to in the delimitation of

2002; the decade-long demarcation of the China-Vietnam land boundary was completed in 2009; citing environmental, cultural, and social concerns, China has reconsidered construction of 13 dams on the Salween River, but energy-starved Burma, with backing from Thailand, remains intent on building five hydroelectric dams downstream despite regional and international protests; Chinese and Hong Kong authorities met in March 2008 to resolve ownership and use of lands recovered in Shenzhen River channelization, including 96-hectare Lok Ma Chau Loop

Refugees and internally displaced persons:
refugees (country of origin): 300,896 (Vietnam) (2011); undetermined (North Korea)
IDPs: undetermined (2014)

Trafficking in persons:
current situation: China is a source, transit, and destination country for men, women, and children subjected to sex trafficking and forced labor; Chinese adults and children are forced into prostitution and various forms of forced labor, including begging and working in brick kilns, coal mines, and factories; women and children are recruited from rural areas and taken to urban centers for sexual exploitation, often trafficked by criminal syndicates or gangs; state-sponsored forced labor continues to be an area of serious concern; Chinese men, women, and children also may be subjected to conditions of sex trafficking and forced

labor worldwide, particularly in overseas Chinese communities; women and children are trafficked to China from neighboring countries, as well as Europe and Africa, for forced labor and prostitution

tier rating: Tier 2 Watch List - China does not fully comply with the minimum standards for the elimination of trafficking; however it is making significant efforts to do so; the government's conflation of human trafficking with other crimes in 2013 made it difficult to assess alw enforcement efforts to investigate and to prosecute trafficking offenses according to international law; authorities did not provide the data needed to ascertain the number of victims identified or assisted or the services provided; the National People's Congress ratified a decision to abolish "reform through labor" (RTL); reports indicate some detainees were released and many RTL camps ceased operations, but others show that some RTL facilities have been converted into different types of detention centers; some North Koeran refugees continued to be forcibly repatriated as illegal economic migrants, despite reports that some were trafficking victims (2014)

Illicit drugs:
major transshipment point for heroin produced in the Golden Triangle region of Southeast Asia; growing domestic consumption of synthetic drugs, and heroin from Southeast and Southwest Asia; source country for methamphetamine and

heroin chemical precursors, despite new regulations on its large chemical industry; more people believed to be convicted and executed fro drug offences than anywhere else in the world, according to NGOs (2008)

www.ingramcontent.com/pod-product-compliance
Lightning Source LLC
Chambersburg PA
CBHW070720180526
45167CB00004B/1552